DEPARTURES

Also by Diane Moore

POETRY:

YOUNG ADULT:

ADULT FICTION:

Silence Never Betrays
Chant of Death
Goat Man Murder
The Maine Event
Nothing for Free

CHILDREN:

The Beast Beelzebufo
The Cajun Express

NON-FICTION:

Iran: In A Persian Market
Their Adventurous Will
Live Oak Gardens
Porch Posts: Memoirs of Porch Sitters
Treasures of Avery Island

DEPARTURES

Diane Marquart Moore

BP

Sewanee Tennessee

Border Press
PO Box 3124
Sewanee Tennessee 37375
www.borderpressbooks.com

ISBN: 9780989864169

Printed in the United States

Cover art by Paul Marquart
Cover design by Martin W. Romero

For Darrell Bourque
who was with me along the way

Diane Marquart Moore

BETWEEN SEASONS

I.
Light blinds the trees,
old branches moving slowly
in a drawn-out day
sullied by the gray ship
of Cumberland mists.
Silver cobwebs build
on the glass,
bringing memories of the dead
filtering through oak branches,
celebrating
the full crew's remains.

Smoke rises,
fills the past,
that window on darkness
and wrong direction,
rain singing the refrain
it was late when you began.

Myths wane,
become the mural
of a daubed landscape,
 a final painting.
The shadow of a pen
flickers on white walls,
dust gathers
in a room that never sleeps,
outside, a yellow leaf

Departures

flutters and falls,
a strange thud on the dry grass.

II.
Dogwoods turn bronze
in the frame of a morning window,
the precipice of October.
Squirrels, runners on rooftops at night,
leave smears of blood
drying on the porch.
What attackers come in the darkness,
a mole thrust out of its tunnel?
a sparrow flying
too close to the glass?

By day, another adventure
begins overhead,
unsettling noises of feet
scurrying toward an abundance of acorns
as if famine is on the wind
and they'll never see a season again.
Trees thin out,
diminish in stature,
and a lake across the road
comes closer.

Crows perch on a wire,
threatening takeover
from their watch tower,
black band on their wings,
death in their yellow eyes.
Nature loads her suitcase
for another life,

Departures

leaving in the dusk
fading colors,
scattering stale bread crumbs.

III.
Some days it matters little
that life has been
a smudged pane
facing the inattentive mountain,
rainstorms fret,
make mud in impassive soil,
base impulses of the psyche
having smeared the glass
of years lying in a trunk,
the hidden sacred in each one.

Now, the aging mind
rushes toward desire
to become clear as the mirror
of a silver lake
glittering in central Florida,
untouched by a blue heron,
head bowed, wading, waiting
on the shore of hunger.

THE NIGHT THEY KILLED AMÉDÉ ARDOIN

Each fold of the accordion
squeezed out the question
why am I here?
In the dark pool of his eyes
loneliness held its secrets,
and the wail of his voice
lingered in the women's ears,
the ones who saw the pain of labor
flickering in those sad eyes.

And they came from miles around—
Basile, Eunice, Opelousas,
drawn by the language
of a Cajun lover,
drawn to the squeeze box
and the short figure
standing on the stage of a juke joint,
while the sky
turned white with lightning
and thunder threatened
that something was done,
everything shrilling in the damp air,
the atmosphere heavy
with the hint of someone fallen.

And in the humid night,
a dog barks,
a white woman takes her handkerchief

14

from a handbag filled with dreams,
wipes the sweat off his brown face.
The music stops,
the question falls out of the folds
of the squeeze box
and he puts his hand
over his mouth,
the high voice, interrupted,
as surprised at the silence
as its listeners,
his head already in the path
of an angry wheel,
the song,
curiously unfaltering,
floating above the bare prairie.

GRANDFATHER PAUL

was tired of living in his body
five years before he died,
a Ford salesman who lost his spiel,
emptied the bowl of his briar pipe
and parked it on the bureau,
but it wasn't tobacco that took him.

He began filling
a wavy green glass with clabber,
crumbling cornbread into the vessel
and calling it supper,
and afterward,
we gathered tomatoes together,
placing them on the kitchen sill
to ripen for an appetite
he no longer had.

Before bedtime,
he'd sit on the floor
his failing body between my knees,
and I raked his head
with a fine-toothed comb,
sprinkling his scalp with Listerine,
scratching his demons away.

The weight of his body complaints
never touched me,
he was the invincible man;
Grandmother Nell, beside him,

16

heard them all,
wore them without replying.

It was the kidneys' failure.
When I was eleven
I no longer heard
the steady stream
splashing into the night pail,
and they took him to the clinic,
where they recorded eight afflictions
that had done their work.

I didn't weep
when his body lay in the parlor,
but after his death,
every night for fifty-one years
I dreamed he returned to us,
telling the same story—
he'd been working in another town,
some far-off place like Canada,
as far as he could go
as long as he could escape
the humid Louisiana nights.

At 62, the age he left us,
 I stopped dreaming about him,
accepted he had left us
for good, finally knew
that none of us
are ever displaced,
we just don't come back.

WHY MARKHAM PLANTED
CAMELLIAS AT AGE 94

They turn brown within a day
'though we think we're cutting them free,
removing them from crowded clusters.
But their tarnish reminds us
they belong on the bush,
can only make a short visit.

The pink camellias bloom
despite their age,
their longing for nurture and water,
the large faces still showy
after February frost,
bees in the nose cones,
leaves pocked with blight,
dark spots marking green boundaries
but leaving us showers of pink,
the way his age
suddenly fell away
as he turned the soil
of a better disposition...
those last days.

Pink camellias
at the edge of the coulee
now confront us each day,
showing us something
we had not realized while he lived,
a story he could not tell:

he planted them deep
before he returned to
the stiffening earth
so they could flower
in wavering light,
so their beauty could prepare us
for the thing he could not name.

HER NAME WAS REALLY NELLIE

but she called herself Sarah Nell,
the renaming a sign
of her "false pride," my father said,
a term I never understood
until I began writing
Ash Wednesday sermons, chides
about pride and humility
not being bedfellows.

She didn't get along with my mother,
a woman whose stocking seams
were never straight,
but she cared for the children
my mother bore,
her conflicted heart
sometimes icing over maternal love.

She carried herself proud,
silk dress swishing down the aisle
of the First Baptist Church,
always worried
we might become careless dressers
or outrageous in behavior,
the even part in her hair
showing pink scalp,
clean as her hardshell scruples,
never went to town barelegged,
wore smocks when cleaning house,
grew pansies in the front yard

for everyone to see,
pruned her hedges each year,
fit in with the landscape
of domestic duty.

She clothed me from birth
until the day I married
and never abandoned the conviction
that my mother married down,
but when she got heart spells
she drank the homemade elderberry wine
with which my father watered
her proud, teetotaling soul.

She died in her sleep,
never having heard
whispered conversation
about how well *she* lived her life,
and when I stand in the pulpit
and preach against my own poetry,
I hear her voice telling the congregation
the old morality tale
of how to live a life,
one that will ever remind you
to keep your stocking seams straight.

SISTER

The photograph is of early morning,
pre-school, tricycle days,
the trike, purple and white,
fancy hand brake,
a streamlined carrier
we boarded to cross
the great divide between fantasy
and a snarling house behind us.
We were headed for New York City,
and she wore a brown dress
with designs of yellow peanuts,
scattered from top button to hem
that we planned to eat
along the way.

We were sidewalk urchins
turned out of doors on wash day;
she was three, and I was six,
and the photo shows us bonded,
settled in arms of love,
my feet dragging ground,
too long for an infantile pinafore,
lambs gamboling across its bodice.

Four years later, one of her legs,
too short for a new bicycle,
caught in the spokes
as she climbed aboard,
slicing a heel to the bone.

I carried her into the house,
her blood trailing on the sidewalk
we had traveled so far together.

My father insisted she heal naturally
and she lay, silent,
a waif on plump pillows,
immobile for six weeks,
long enough for the wound
to lodge in her heart,
the benign neglect of a parent
forcing her forever inward,
unlike water
receiving a wound from a pebble
and closing around it at once,
her heart was unwilling to mend...

She died in the fifth decade of her life,
asphyxiated in a closed garage.

We had not traveled together for years.

My granddaughter painted
a copy of the photo,
and I hung it at the foot of my bed
where I can see
how we once pedaled
on sidewalks leading to sisterly love,
where I can remember
how dispossessed we all feel
when no one tends our wounds,

Departures

and we cannot bear ourselves.

Diane Marquart Moore

WHEN BROTHER LEFT HOME,

the street received him
as no one ever had,
the dark canon of its tenants
cradling his desire to be free.
There had been demons in the chimney
and ashes on the altar of the Church,
he had tried obeisance to Mary,
novenas and The Knights,
and they had received him not.

We sent him to the asylum
and he disappeared in the night,
detectives said someone had killed him,
thrown him into Lake Ponchartrain.

They watched for floating corpses.

Check his credit card, I told them,
it's a plastic compass without needle,
the family train always moves West,
we're fond of the sound of rails.

They checked his charges to California,
discovered him sheltered in San Diego
where he promised to live forever.
He took up residence in shelters,
hospitals, doorways in the street,
the king of madness and muscatel
granting his every wish.

25

And the last call came to me,
the streets of Chicago had claimed him
as no one ever had,
the dark canon of its tenants
fulfilling sixty years of desire
to finally break free.

Diane Marquart Moore

YOUR DARK FACE

filled with the "anti-urge,"*
caught me with a look
as if it were always raining,
eyes drooping
in self-inspired melancholia,
the secret face
a determinant of loneliness.

Failed the first grade twice.
When asked to read aloud,
your heart thrumming in alarm
against your polo shirt,
too late they discovered the dyslexia

you tried to cure by running away,
a ten-year old boy with a friend
hungry for adventure,
paddling an old Joe boat
against the currents
of the Bogue Chitto River
Huck and Tom arrested in development.

Your mother signed you into the Air Force—
the father you never had,
taught you to read,
a wounded boy hiding away
among blue uniforms,
emerging as a man.
You still viewed

27

the world's message
upside down,
telling stories about the U.S.
being settled by transmogrified creatures
who flew in from outer space,
about reading Ayn Rand
and feeling your mind become unconflicted,
Sane.

When you graduated from college
I breathed a sigh of relief.
You had settled in the sunlight.
But your wife deserted you,
you lost three jobs,
put your arms into a strait jacket
and left your brain
on the back screen porch
with my drunken father.

When you woke up
he was gone,
your brother, a rabid dog
chased you up on a roof
and you climbed down
to fellow insanity,
walked twenty miles in August heat,
looking for work that would fit
someone who seemed to be
but was not,
your heart bursting
at the finish line

of the VA office
before you could reach the arms
of those blue uniforms
that had welcomed you at 16.

Dead at 52.
Headed for the planet
that had beamed you alive,
those strange beings welcoming you
into your own at last.

*Jane Kenyon in *"Having It Out With Melancholy: I. From the Nursery." Collected Poems of Jane Ken*yon.

Departures

TEACHER, THIRD GRADE

You wrote on the black wall
of my brain,
a surface
touched only lightly,
a hesitant organ waiting
for you to imprint
in fine lines
the passion of excellence.

I would have been without song
had you not given me
the power of searching for unknowns:
Longfellow, Xochimilco, a flower pollinating—
the fruits of learning.
I surrendered to a pointer
tapping the chalky surface,
a blackboard
claiming my intrepid mind.

Years later, I found your number,
and you answered,
a frail voice of 98 years,
a tenuous lifeline an hour away.
You did not remember me.

But your red hair still flames in my poems,
you who made me
take the stairs,
you who died the year after

I called.

But not before I told you
how many doors
you had unlatched,
how your raised hands
taught me
the art of pondering
how to use the invisible
web of mind.

THEY LOVED SHIRLEY TEMPLE'S LOCKS

My hair has always had inertia
but my aunts loved curly hair,
they wrapped me in pin curls
and rolled away my childhood,
gentle hands on my neck,
solicitude in bobbie pins;
now and then a yank,
a brush to untangle sleep knots,
those hands swift in lankness,
pinning, rolling, rolling, pinning
until they discovered the magic
of Toni home perms.

And when they were ready
to go into the ground,
before they went into oblivion,
I stepped back from a longing
to feel their hands pulling, pinning,
stroking my shorn white locks,
thought I heard both of them,
coiffed and curled for eternity,
sigh with grand relief
but looking as if they wanted
a bobbie pin placed
in each of their wrinkled hands
on the satin pillow
beside them,
hair being known to grow

after you reach the other side.

Departures

FOR MORRIS RAPHAEL (RAFOUL)

It was a reminder
of your death in hottest July,
the sight of your name on the plaque
of a crumbling building in Natchez,
Mississippi,
and the withered fig tree drooping
in the dry straw of winter,
symbol of knowing good and evil
planted over eight decades ago,

wild grape vines wrapping their arms
around your daughter's memories.

It was the light blazing
in the canvas of sky,
scarred branches forming
the skeleton of a life,
calling your name — Rafoul,
a man of the river town
who stood in the shadow
of white columns:
the offspring of rich soil and cotton,
slave traders, peddlers, gamblers
bringing their saddle bags
and mingling beneath the bluff

near the River
where hell once raged.

You never knew that country
on the shores of the Mediterranean
your father left behind,
Lebanon,
the place called "mountain of snow."
But you left your own native soil
to pass through the hills
and settle on the banks
of a mystical bayou

where history became your applause.

You inscribed your last book
to *preserve history,*
a noble contribution,
then put down your pen and died,
a century and a half
after a War Between the States
the cotton kingdom birthed,
in the shadow of the white columns
and the fig tree your father planted
from a branch of the mother plant,

sweet fruit you once savored,
sweet fruit you left us.

MATERNAL CLAIMS

I am the daughter
who mothered you.
I honor your legacy:
the excitement of travel,
camping out in Texas,
the western encampment,
foolish desire planted
in a place never far
from me and the mind
growing in me.

I reel with hunger.
I feed on memory,
I see you in khaki,
stained and rumpled pullover,
hunched over a campfire.
You, entranced with survival--
scavenging experience
and the voice in stories,
voice drowned out often
by father's shouting,
voice giving me my voice.

Climbing granite cliffs in Hill Country
among the cedar scrub,
you stood on ground
made sacred simply
because you were standing
on it, priestess

of the Edwards Plateau,
dreaming dreams repeating
themselves in you
and repeating themselves
in me.

After you died, I found the shirt
crumpled in the chest father built--
blue coffin holding family scrapbooks.
The shirt -- tattered, bleached out,
a reminder of those sunny days
moving West,
locks of your childrens' hair
folded in its pockets,
and I heard you singing
"A lady they called the gypsy."
I saw you waving
at windmills of happiness
spinning near Llano, Texas.

I am your daughter,
a prodigal,
but your daughter nonetheless.
I thumb through
stacks of postcards
you collected, you climbing
the Guadalupe Range,
10,000 feet above the tent.
You finally pitched in a place
that unsettled you.
Today, I am thumbing

through your wanderlust
and how it stirs in me.

I hear again
your calls for help,
telephone jangling
four times a day, shrill
tales about father's drinking.
Your asking me
to give you a sign.
You say you want
God's sobriety
in the wombs of your children.
You say you want
your own will and theirs
unshaken.

Looking out at me
from the mirror of biology,
you: my mother, my daughter,
me: your mother, your daughter
my daughters, their mother,
their mother, the daughters.
We are laying claim
on each other
and to each other
in flickering reflections,
in this dual existence,
in this dual endurance.

DOROTHY WANTED TO BE A CARDINAL

You were buried in the summer
wearing a jacket with red buttons.
I've written many poems
predicting your return,
a cardinal invading my privacy,
the Great Unconscious moaning
at your resurrections.

You drift up again and again.

A dawdler landing on my lawn,
you were the mother lost to me
until you died
and returned on red wing,
albeit the color of male birds
who tortured you on earth.

You pass from sight
while I stand at the window
watching your many ascensions,
soaring beyond the suffering
you lived with us,
but bearing the same name—
Dorothy, "a gift of god,"
released,
wearing your protective mantle...
the feathers of red delight.

JUST DESSERTS

He wore the beard,
an overgrown yard
framing his terrible face,
called himself a Jewish patriarch —
something he traced to Alsace Lorraine
only at my urging,
touting that the angels
had declared him a prophet
who could rise above
the curse of drink
while turning pages of *The Rubaiiyat*
as if it contained the wisdom
that would restore all of us,

the wine of his life
oozing drop by drop *
and him raking up the needles
of his overgrown yard
so he wouldn't know
they were his own years
falling one by one. *

His sorrows lay under the pines
that he invited us to view
at family meals,
forestalling the arguments
raging above the last piece
of chocolate pie,
which he claimed,

40

ignoring the family buzzing
like the local sawmill,
and savoring every greedy bite.

One tear he shed
when I blessed his hands
at death,
and sometimes when the wind
blows the right way,
his recitations rise
above the skull
of his shrunken head,
claiming it was not wine that
robbed him of his cloak of honor,*
for after all, he turned down the glass,
dry, in his last years.
He said it was the gnawing thought
of his family's hunger
that dishonored him,
their lust for a comfortable life...
and just a small sliver
of that creamy chocolate pie.

**The Rubaiyat of Omar Khayyam*

INSPIRATION

Being brought up to fear authority
I was not surprised
when my fingers
trembled on the keys,
fell between them,
ten thumbs wide
in one finger space
when M.L. Shaw stood
behind my desk
watching me,
the mistress of un-coordination.

Each smudged carbon copy
was the belt on my back,
my left hand never knew
what the right hand was doing,
I was be-handed by an ancient Royal.
How could I ever become a writer
with such uncertain script?

I never cut class.
She never rebuked me.

She held no ruler to my knuckles
but her raven-colored hair
with the precise side part,
matching sweater and skirt outfits,
the way she applied lipstick
with the little finger of her left hand

42

to make that prim crimson mouth,
placed limits on my ambition.

She breathed exactingness.

And then came exaltation
the day I read that
the titans of modern lit
typed with one finger,
committed strikeovers,
and never made carbon copies
of their work.

She sent me into the world
keyed into an uncertain vocation,
but before she died,
inscribed a fat collection
of Shakespeare's plays
in her flowing, exacting hand:
"I hope you'll always think kindly of me."
And my skills gained a pace,
my hands reached a standard,
the classroom was eclipsed.

I clocked out
at 80 words per minute.

GODMOTHER DORA

She braided her hair
every morning,
fastening it with sprung hairpins
on top of her cautious head,
was chauffeured up to Roanoke
on the front seat of an aging Buick
twice a week,
wearing a brown hat and veil,
gloves, sheer stockings,
and size three shoes.

She had no daughters of her own,
always said she'd leave me
a house, bone china,
money, silver,
a universe of wealth—
the Victorian thing to do
for another woman.
A woman, as Virginia Woolf said,
should have not only
a room of her own,
but the means to maintain it.

Yet, she wanted me to agree
never to divorce,
stay faithful
to a ruptured marriage,
or I'd be unlikely
to attain heaven.

Diane Marquart Moore

It was Aunt Ide's counsel
that wives must endure
the long visit of abuse.

Someone will carry me out of here,
I told her,
if I stay with him
it will be the end of my time.
I'm not fond of cold light
and morning terror,
my children cling to me,
frightened birds not ready to fly,
like crouching dogs
under a wobbly table
we eat the crusts
of no love, no peace,
live under a gray stone.
And I won't stay any longer.

I moved past my frayed hopes,
divorced,
five years before her death.
She died one June morning
in the canopied Mallard bed,
Victorian morals intact,
a cancer in the stomach
had eaten away
her own endurance.

And she left me nothing
except the unwarranted message,

45

Departures

"you were always too impulsive,"
a sentence that still shadows
the mild days of June,
as I sit,
a woman of freedom and leisure
...in a room of my own.

THE UNCLES

Uncle Tony bought me a plastic sword
with gold painted handle,
a dollar's worth of fancy
at the Washington Parish Fair.
He shied away from picture taking
with anyone,
even his infant niece.
But Uncle Jimmy loved adoration
and allowed a Kodak shot
of him squatting beside me
as I hugged the famous stuffed bear
named for him...
a character in my father's bedtime stories.

Uncle Tony took me riding
in the countryside near Mt. Hermon
to see his aged father,
a cliché of the redneck farmer,
still drinking from a tin pail
on a porch rail of his tenant cabin,
spat in the red dust of his yard
and frightened me out of
ever taking a ride in the country
with him again.

Uncle Tony was tall, looked like
a Vaseline hair tonic ad,
his dun colored hair slicked back
with no part;

Departures

Uncle Jimmy had natural wavy hair
and avoided brushes;
both men were handsome,
smoked Camel cigarettes,
men of the 40's who believed
smoking was sophistication.

My uncles were mill men,
one working in a paper mill,
the other in a sugar mill;
both came up from poverty
and the Great Depression,
rubbed their sharp beards
against my infant face
for at least five years of my life.

When I became a teenager,
Uncle Tony couldn't remember
carrying me on his shoulder
or holding my hand when
we walked together,
both men seemed uncomfortable
after I reached puberty
and my parents started calling me
"a little American beauty,"
kept their distance,
as if I had become unlovable
by virtue of a good appearance.

They died before they reached sixty,
both succumbing to lung cancer,

and I missed their funerals.
But they missed most of my life.
We were a family belonging to a species
that spent little time together,
were among the dispossessed,
had too many secrets
to manage the intimacy,
too many of us not being
what we appeared to be.

POPS

owned a dried up rice field
near Lacassine, Louisiana,
and a rundown boarding establishment
built like an Iowa farmhouse,
it was all that remained
of the Marquart Land Company,
which bought and laid out
the town of Lake Arthur.

He maintained the family tradition
of ignoring tragedies pressing in
to focus on some aspect of art —
a music note, finely carved furniture,
words in a notebook,
a daub of paint on a canvas,
some concentration of heart and mind
to avoid the overhang of suffering.

But his was the art of observation
practiced from the post of a recliner
he built in a day before Big Boys,
feet propped on a broken footstool,
watching the boarders eat, drink,
play cards on a long table,
smoke curling from his Meerschaum pipe,
each cloud like a cartoon bubble
with words scratched within,
"can't be trusted,"
"heavy drinker,"

"possible arsonist,"
"won't pay on time,"
and worst of all — "womanizer."

He passed this on to Moms
who tucked his warnings
into a patent leather purse,
smoothed down the Orlon dress
that had hiked up on a behind
carrying 300-pounds
and went on playing cards
with all of his "observations."

In the afternoons at two sharp,
he'd make strong coffee
in a white enamel French pot
to wake himself up,
a German who didn't believe
that hard work won all,
sired three boys who did.

Dressed like a factory worker,
khaki shirt, khaki pants
never ironed,
he gave his life to observation,
philosophical reflection,
passing on to my father nine words
from a lifetime of looking on:
"trite sayings are the
distilled wisdom of the ages."

Departures

At the last, he kept to himself
on a second story sleeping porch,
leaving behind his dreams
and an economy of words,
a pair of khaki pants
hanging on a nail,
pockets turned inside out.

Diane Marquart Moore

SISTER'S BLUE BABY,

the only boy among three girls,
was buried in blue satin

in a tiny steel box
that held the porcelain body

and a heart that struggled
against death

before his time;
his crippled valves

leaking a love
never expressed...

 and only his mother felt.

BILLY AND BIRD

When I read about Billy Scarlett dying,
I felt as though Bird Parker
had died again;
Bird, dying at 34,
an old man's body
playing the last notes
in a score of cirrhosis,
pneumonia, bleeding ulcers,
heart failure.

Bird — hippy idol, blues man,
uncompromising bebopper king
of the 20th century,
a wild man I saw through Billy's eyes,
heard through Billy's own sax
jamming its destiny
in an overflowing ashtray,
booze, and pot.

I remember a gig
one sultry August night
in Baton Rouge, Louisiana,
a jam session at the Bonanza,
Billy slamming his sax
to the ground,
shattering the keys
because he'd broken the night
with notes that squawked,
tone trash he said the Yardbird

would've tuned out.

I never heard Billy's idol play onstage
but I had a front row seat
in Billy's living room
the time he spun a platter
of Bird shaking his sax
when a sour note came out,
shaking and chirping
until sweet and somber notes
from the throat of an immense wind
pierced the gloom;

no cooing doves,
but notes blasted
as if they sought the ceiling
in a closed nightclub
on Bleecker Street;
Bird playing to an empty room
while neon lights
flashed in my brain
and the sound went off
into the rafters,
gritting its teeth.

When I read about Billy dying,
not three hours away
in another Tennessee city,
time was, I thought,
when we thumbed our noses
at "moldy figs"

and listened to the music
those figs couldn't play,
contrafact, jazz solos,
ears humming with horn.

Billy and Bird
phrasing and innovating
Blues for Alice,
K.C. Blues,
and, oh yes,
you could slow dance
to their *Lover Man*;

Billy and Bird
hustling on the street
when the money gave out,
bebopping their way
to the heaven of Birdland,
home of jazz angels;
fingering notes that flapped their wings,
altering chords with a wailing amen,
 playing those twelve bar blues.

Diane Marquart Moore

OBIT FACT CHECKER

And when you depart this world,
will your mourners run
an Instant Checkmate online,
to see if your epitaph/obit
is accurate, checking the record
that shows nothing is sacred
and most things are not so secretive
in this visible kingdom...
this inventory of all you left behind:

parking and speeding tickets,
citations for drunken driving,
juvenile misdemeanors,
divorce proceedings;
whether you graduated at the bottom
of your high school class,
or even passed through college portals;

the 35-year mortgage
on the three bedroom home you bought
and mortgaged again in your old age;
the diseases you suffered through,
blood stains and heavy eyes,
anti-depressants and sleeping pills
you swallowed so you could endure
the failures in business ventures,
your laughter muffled by the cries
of crows flying in starless skies,
your prayers for money

unheard by the averted ears of the one
who created this game of chance;

the sentence that you never served
as president of any civic endeavor,
you, an officer on the road to nowhere;
but the slight mention of your stint
shrieking in a church choir
an opera in which time pressed
the diminuendo of voice;

that you bore children,
one child becoming an addict
always on a night shift,
the other, married to a bum
in a house thick with dust;

the suggestion that your last words
were not publishable,
everything, anything that might
put another spike in your frozen heart,
throw a shadow on the life
you lived as a law-abiding citizen
who deserved the epitaph of "Dutiful"
etched on your lavish tombstone.
Requiescat in pace.

Diane Marquart Moore

LET THE TREES ANSWER

The landscape is one of broken branches,
tan leaves withering in rain,
maps of lichen clinging to tree trunks.
What crooked branch
and seared grass
held out such promise
that we would circle
around yesterday
and settle the blood

grown thicker further South
where we came up from lush spring
trusting that these deaths
would become vaporous forms,
float over the bluff

into the valley of Cowan?
That we would stop asking
why we came here —
surely not to be stranded
or lose our way again.
Too soon, we will become Other.

The yellow explosions of flowers,
watchful trees,
rustle in evening silence.
They are still heavy with questions:
where did all those years go?
Roots gnarl deep.

Departures

But will we, too, vanish forever?

ALL THEIR DEPARTURES

Spring comes,
a psychic cleansing,
lavender petals of Japanese magnolia
sigh in the March wind;
there is this sudden divergence,
an opening of windows
to let the memories out.

I step outside to spring light
where there is nothing greener
than the first crop of grass
dusted with white clover,
blooms, brazen in the sun,
scent the air.

These family passings,
the weather of winter storms,
I stop missing all of them,
their secrets forced back into darkness,
their points of departure felt.
I no longer admit dead reckonings,
the faces have appeared often enough.
I am not anxious to see them again,
they have left enough
of themselves with me.

POSTSCRIPT

The old man, near 90,
mans a fruit stand

at the edge of Cowan, Tennessee;
watermelon season,

pumpkin season,
during the worst kind of winter,

stands, hands in his pockets,
announcing to anxious buyers:

"I'm just glad to be on this side of the grass..."